RIP THE SCRIPT | CONTEMPLATE | REINVIGORATE

*Update **Your** Thinking*

J. MONTEE

RIP THE SCRIPT

CONTEMPLATE

REINVIGORATE

Bring the background chatter

toward

the forefront to be examined

for

enlightenment and correction

CONTENTS

* * *

WORDS OF:

Hope

Experience

Fun

Spirit

Recovery

Wisdom

Time

• • •

Words to live by

Think by

Love by

Say by

• • •

Take a heaping plate full

Buffet style

Go back for seconds

Every day if you like

Do you like Fortune Cookies?

INTRODUCTION

The purpose of this book is to utilize the ideas herein, to stay and excel at being well. *I'm not a professional, just a thinker, observer, and experiencer.*

In wanting to readily relate these ideas in an effective long-lasting way, and to visually mold them into our life, I found it necessary to use sometimes windy wording, expressions, and feelings, while at other times, short and direct sayings.

"Thinking it" is not as important as saying and expressing what we learn. When we say and express illuminating ideas, we can "Say Well." When we hear ideas said well, it may help us be well.

Think all you want, but not too much! In this book I am not going to get too "psycho-pathetic."

There is frank, pull no punches, commentary with no sugar coating, so fasten your seat belt.

Yes, we can have and need to have fun too!

I hope there is enough material here for everyone. There is much for "recovering" and "recovered" people. They know who they are, and others may find that they qualify too. If not, substitute or glean what you can.

So don't think about it.
Act about it.
May all
"Say Well"

. . .

A LITTLE BIT
ABOUT ME

Growing up I felt I was treated harshly, persecuted by an angry father who was scary. He never had time for me. He was always working. The most frustrating and confusing thing was he worked right downstairs, in the same house we lived in. The looks I received from my father were sometimes brutal and scary. I had to vie for his attention. I was an annoyance but I still craved him being present for me in my life. Damn it, I was his son!

He always pointed out everything I did wrong or thought I did wrong. In hindsight I wish I would have said to him, "Correct me if I'm right!"

My father liked being alone. He just needed somebody to be alone with. My mother.

Not being able to feel good about myself, I would come to look to find a "special" woman to win over. This only worked in the short term. Being that I still didn't like *me*, I would then view her as inadequate for accepting me. My unhappiness would cause me to point the finger at her.

Some people can have the same upbringing and become unscathed by the day-to-day occurrences I went through. Everyone is different, or hard-wired differently, so to speak.

These are my experiences. They may not be yours. This is what I have found from my experiences, both past and post upbringing. These are things I have lived and learned. Some, I have left behind.

The Apartment

When I had my first apartment I felt free. I had everything under control.

I was going out with this girl I met at a bar. She had some friends that were moving out and didn't want to wait for the lease to be up so I subleased the apartment from them and forked over the security they would have gotten. It was real cheap. This couple was going to Minnesota, I think to become drug and alcohol counselors!

My vacuum cleaner was an electric broom and I think it put out more dust than it sucked up. But I had everything under control. My clothes washing consisted of dumping the colors and whites together. Very efficient! My undershirts would be shades of beige and gray. Hey, I wore them "under" my shirts so who could see? Everything was under control.

I used to blast the stereo system with the windows open. I had four speakers and just blasted them and had a good time.

The girl I met at the bar broke up with me and I met this other girl, at the same bar of course. I went to live with this girl kinda sorta. I was going out with her for a few months. She was a bartender and things were really under control now. I kept the apartment as a backup. I wound up staying there on and off when things got crazy. I had several plants. I didn't go in there for what seemed like a month once and almost all of them died.

In the refrigerator, the vegetable bin was perfect because I could put the beer cans in sideways on the bottom. They all fit down there really nice and neat so everything was under control.

I do have one plant to this day that I sort of brought back to life. It's a Swedish Ivy. It's a reminder. We both lived, just barely.

• • •

RELATIONSHIPS

(MY TAKE)

When first interested in a potential mate, the things that seem cute can become "a-cutely" annoying as time goes on.

. . .

"Hey, Sugar Free, you're so sweet, and
not bad for me!" Isn't that sweet?

"It's not just what I see, it's who you be!" Isn't that sweet?

. . .

It takes me over a year to grieve the loss of a relationship.
Even one lasting less than that. Tough stuff.

. . .

Poison that has been sweetened is more deadly. You
drink more. It could be women, could be booze.

I can annoy women,

I can annoy men,

I am an equal opportunity annoyer!

. . .

In relationships, we have differences. Most of these shouldn't make a difference.

. . .

If you get into relationships fast, a relationship *"fast"* may be beneficial.

Always good to cleanse and detox.

. . .

"The Four Honesties"

Communicate, share, and the ways we perceive:

1. How I believe my partner sees me

2. How I see myself

3. How I believe my partner believes I see her

4. How I see my partner

. . .

Peripheral Perception is the observing of oneself from the perspective of being observed, and acting accordingly.

. . .

Perception of others based on gossip can be like secondhand smoke. You don't always know where it's coming from, but you are affected.

. . .

People can sense when they are being judged. This judgmental attitude could have arisen from hearing Gossip, the G word.

. . .

Do not despair too long for there may be only one of her, but there are many shes as in the wise saying about plenty of fish in the sea. (I'm a man so I wrote about a woman. Feel free to substitute.)

. . .

In relationships, what seems like an ending may
just be the beginning of a new chapter.

. . .

Codependent tidal wave:

Don't look to get high on a person. It will
take you up and slam you down.

. . .

Need help? Look for me. *Need* me? Look for help!

Unhealthy dependency.

. . .

If one doesn't know what one wants in life, they are always
going to be wanting. They will most likely seek the wrong
things and then proceed to blame who or whatever is
closest, including the world, for their circumstances.

. . .

As a guy, I used to be a *guyser*. I could blow up when
I got angry. Now I have a different outlook.

Gals were usually *gushers*. When they got angry, tears gushed.

* * *

Guys don't understand what gals are saying.

They just hear what they are seeing.

* * *

Pushing letters with my fingertips instead of speaking words
with my two lips is the missing ingredient in TEXTING!

* * *

Good relationships take the two right people.

I built a good shelf out of natural wood.

It was empty at first, just waiting to be filled with books.

The books had to be the right kind,
special, not just any books.

* * *

To Relationship or not to Relationship? That is the question.

. . .

The only way to keep her may be to let her go… let her go…

. . .

Talk things out rather than stuff things in.

. . .

Scary thoughts:

I'm frightened about this new relationship.

If it doesn't work out I'll be single and alone.

On the other hand if it does work out, I won't be single or alone. Both are scary thoughts!

. . .

If you can't do being *single* well, you're probably not going to do being a *couple* well.

. . .

Sometimes you just have to say,
"If you can't move on, move over."

◦ ◦ ◦

Are we starting off this love affair right or is it starting us off?

◦ ◦ ◦

Hard to change what I said by what I say.

Once sent out of mouth, pen, or keyboard, it's too late.

◦ ◦ ◦

Conversating or convergazing? One leads to romance!

◦ ◦ ◦

Too long alone. Become ingrown!

◦ ◦ ◦

Friends *first*, usually *lasts*!

. . .

Why an older man is better for a younger woman, maybe.

What is the difference between the way a 45 year old man and a 58 year old man feels about a 44 year old woman? Well, there is no difference. However a married 58 year old man knows the likelihood of leaving his wife for a 44 year old is not feasible. The 45 year old married man may try it and does have a shot. To the 58 year old single guy, if he marries a woman of 44, to him she will always be a young catch! So younger women, consider it!

. . .

Young, single, and not knowing *exactly* what they want, when they get together, they grow together.

. . .

Older singles, in knowing *exactly* what they want when they get together, don't easily compromise, which can lead to relationship demise.

. . .

Sometimes when a misunderstanding occurs and I try to quiet the storm, I only make waves!

. . .

Listen? Nope, you don't want to hear from me. You just want to hear from you.

. . .

Relationships nowadays have gone the way of silverware and china. They are now plastic forks and paper plates, disposable.

. . .

Holiday Hauntings

The brain remembers but you don't.

I'm talking about those weird subterranean feelings
that come up during the holidays, especially when with
family or that special person on that special day.

All kinds of uncomfortable, irritating, fearful
feelings can come up just under the surface.
It's those Holiday Hauntings. Being aware
takes the air out of these little beasties.

Admitting them to someone or just stating in general
that the Holiday Weirdies are hitting you and "it's not
about you," they can help you get through them.

• • •

Relating to others is a dance. When you wear
steel-toed construction boots how can the dance
go well? A little vulnerability and authenticity
makes for a more intimate dance.

• • •

If I say the right thing in the wrong way, then I said the wrong thing! An example of right becoming wrong.

* * *

Before you say something that may offend, even if you want to help, try it on for size, as they say. Imagine someone saying it to you, "How would you possibly feel?"

* * *

You change a little
I change a little
we then both meet
in the middle

* * *

My ideal woman is the one I can bring over to meet mom and then take home to my place! Such a woman!

* * *

I am me and she is she
The same
Neither of us will ever be

. . .

That wall of emotional protection has
a price. Less love, less affection.

. . .

Were you guilted most of your life and
now you are guilting it back?

. . .

Placing someone on a pedestal runs the risk
of placing yourself curbside at times.

. . .

**Conflict between the way things are
and the way you want them to be.**

With Reality on one side of the gauge
Desires on the other
The closer the needle moves
Toward Reality
The more Peace and Contentment
Will be available.

* * *

Taking on responsibility in order to control. "It's my fault!"

"If I can blame myself for things not going well in a
relationship, then *I* can *change* and keep us together."

This is delusional thinking! The other person has
a part in it as well. I am separate from that.

* * *

You cannot make new Old Friends. Try
and keep those tried and true ones.

* * *

Who do you think I am and who do I think you are?

· · ·

A strong personality is fine, just don't aim it at me!

· · ·

It's one thing to say something that's appropriate.
It's another to say it inappropriately.

· · ·

With some women there was magic between us.

We just never performed any tricks together.

· · ·

This online dating seems to some akin to a mail
order catalog. They forever browse thinking a
made to order date will appear after skipping
over so many, especially me. Well, shock, we are
looking too! Look over me, I will overlook you.

· · ·

AGNOSTIC THOUGHTS & RATIONAL THOUGHTS

(I WAS ONCE AGNOSTIC)

Rear-view Reasoning is when some outcome (agreeable with the rationalizer) is now looked back upon with certain parts being excluded (selective denial) in order to create some order as to the outcome.

* * *

We initiate

Procreate

Masturbate

Ate great

Disintegrate

* * *

When I was very young I asked my parents how
the grass and the dirt and the trees and the sky and
the sun all got here. They said God made it.

Why didn't they just tell me "We don't know, it was here
when we got here!" (I'm not an agnostic anymore.)

• • •

I have found from my own experience reading scientific
literature written by atheists for the most part with the
theme of disproving God, that there is a disconnect.
Coupled with that theme is that such a high percentage of
scientists (about 60 percent, with the highest percentage
being The National Academy of Science with about 90
percent) are atheist or agnostic. The "smarter" you are, the
less God is believed in. If these "smart guys" who know so
much about how the universe works can't "figure out God,"
so to speak, then they figure God out. They figure God out
of being, period! Within their realm of thought, if there
is no scientific answer then there is no God. Pure logic?

• • •

Scientists use the argument that if the "sun stopped" (earth stopped rotating) as in the Bible, buildings would fall, we would fall, oceans would overtake land with giant tidal waves, earthquakes would ensue, and so, basically, devastation. They laugh at the thought and use it as proof God couldn't be because this event is not survivable, to say the least.

I used to "buy" this when under the agnostic spell. Problem is the scientists and experts are under the spell too, thinking that God is also under the restriction and limits of Newtonian laws and quantum physics. What is to stop God from suspending and reordering the physical character of things in any way, shape, or form that is to God's liking? That would be called a Miracle.

* * *

Changing the material "world." Things happening
out of the ordinary laws of nature. Nature created
by God, albeit over deep time. A God all powerful
with no beginning and no end! Wow! That
ought to blow the minds of the physicists.

. . .

The famous genius scientist Freeman Dyson said, "An
awareness of our smallness may help to redeem us from
the arrogance which is the besetting sin of scientists."

. . .

EGO

Wherever I go, Ego! The need is to get the "I" out of here! I'm all I'd up!

* * *

Just admit you don't know how, or you would have done it by now!

* * *

Two pitfalls:

1. We think we are very special.

2. We think we are not worth mentioning.

* * *

Ego Drink

I call it a C.C. Sour

I can become inebriated on vainglory.

It starts off with a double shot of 100 proof "*Certainty*,"
immediately followed by a large glass of clear "*Conviction.*"
This drinking binge is not worth the hangover of the
emptiness inside, and the souring of people around me.

. . .

If we don't get to unload we will probably get loaded!

. . .

Learn from someone who has the experience.

Do you want to learn farming or house building from
someone who *paints* barns and houses? That's your choice.

. . .

These two words I like. "I know." These two, "I don't."

. . .

The more I feed the ego the bigger its stomach
gets and the more food it needs.

I'll keep it on a diet, thank you.

⁎ ⁎ ⁎

Someone asked what "self centered" is about. I told
them that it was a club consisting of one member,
who wonders why nobody else wants to join.

⁎ ⁎ ⁎

My ego can't be overcome by my ego no matter how strong
it gets. It can be overcome by asking God. God's grace.

⁎ ⁎ ⁎

When I run my life on feeling better than everyone
else, eventually I begin to feel worse, much worse.
This occurs by slowly becoming unraveled and
suddenly disconnected from the human race, alone,
in the dark and cold, outside of existence.

⁎ ⁎ ⁎

My ego is still alive, it's just not as lively, which is good, otherwise it could prove deadly if it gets overinflated.

. . .

Full of themselves

When someone is full of themselves, why is it that I want to throw up? I want to throw them up, like getting rid of something that is nauseating.

. . .

There are those who tend to have a warped sense, not only of the world, but of self.

Eventually with work and good counsel they come to find they are not that bad,

not that good,
not that weird,
not that normal,
not that unique
not perfect after all!

. . .

When your ego is up too high, you put God down.

. . .

Superiority/Inferiority complex.

Feeling superior puts one on top of the world
till it is realized one is not the greatest which
summarily puts you on a free fall to the bottom,
looking up, feeling inferior. This won't do. Time
to feel superior! And so on and on and on…

Find the middle. You may look up a bit and
you may look down a bit. Here, you are.

. . .

Aggravation saturation!

Some people have expectations. I tended
to have *demandtations*!

. . .

Viewed the world through twisted, colored glasses.

. . .

When I tried to run my life on pure self will, I ruined it. "I" am the problem. When I take the "I" and place it after the "u" in run, it spells ruin for me!

. . .

Give up *on yourself.* Self is the problem. Give it up to God. That is the way out.

. . .

Sometimes what you think and I think are different thinks!

TIME

I only have to do this for one day at a time.

* * *

Every moment is an ending. Every moment is a beginning.

Every moment is a beginning. Every moment is an ending.

* * *

I cannot accumulate time. I can only
go through it. Experience it.

* * *

Time doesn't add up.

* * *

Let's fast backward to another time.
Now let's get out of here!

* * *

In order to get somewhere,
I have to go somewhere.

* * *

Slow as snails.

* * *

The longer life gets, the shorter it gets.

* * *

In one second everything could change for good, or
not. Life can be lived and appreciated in the second.

We may not get another second. That is, a second chance.

* * *

New love: every day is like a week.

Lost love: every day is like a year.

. . .

"Youthlessness" is no longer
a hinderance to my happiness.

. . .

We can never look at "Discontinuous Time" in
the same light as Continuous Time because
we will make light of Continuous Time.

. . .

SAY WELL

At any given time

In any given moment

Under any circumstance

For whatever reason

I don't have to drink

That's what Continuous Time speaks to.

* * *

Life moves forward.

When the sun starts rising in the west, then
I'll start worrying about yesterday.

* * *

I wasted a lot of time on the bar stool. I thought
it was time well wasted, at the time.

* * *

"How now brown cow" was a calf but not anymore!

* * *

Let's face it.

Until then, it's now!

* * *

You can postpone living in the moment but then you will
have deprived yourself of having lived in the recent past!

* * *

The sound of death is deafening.

* * *

Lots of the time, I wasted my mind with
the time I spent dwelling in the past and
prospecting in the nonexistent future.

* * *

We are a collection of moments

Gone

Memories stored and

This

Moment after all

. . .

After a time the memory of one said
person fades into "*Forgottenhood.*"

. . .

About The Now:

The Now is being relegated to the past
as the future flows forward.

. . .

WISE TIME

Very confused and left out growing up.

I think I always wanted a "do over"

That's what we kinda get here.

. . .

I need an organized mind.

. . .

Emotionalism can lead to wrong choices
and harm us if we act on the feelings.

So then: Your Wits can save your Grits!

. . .

My frame of mind depends on how I frame my mind.

. . .

Look at the good in life: feel good. Look
at the bad in life: feel bad.

. . .

Instead of thinking about things, get going about things.

. . .

Know what you like and like what you
know about what you like.

. . .

Live in this moment and enjoy because trying
to live in moments that haven't transpired is
futile and removes the reality of the now.

. . .

Sometimes I say what I'm thinking, but
don't always think what I'm saying!

. . .

What is not realized is not lost.

What is lost can be realized too late.

* * *

Verbal Tailgating

When someone speaking speeds and tailgates
their speech, the effect is one long mess of dented,
twisted, unrecognizable words. Slow it down or
you keep the flow *of misunderstanding* going.

* * *

When you go through it

You won't have to go back to it.

* * *

I used to be very optimistic regarding my negative
outlook. Things almost always seemed to work
out for the worst. Just as I predicted.

* * *

Obviously there is a reason. However, the
reason is not always obvious.

· · ·

The drive to arrive

Having arrived it's not enough

We take another drive

Only to arrive and decide

We need more

It's never enough

So we drive until we ultimately find we are out of gas

It never lasts

· · ·

I've heard it said smart people learn from their mistakes. Wise people learn from others' mistakes. So "my way": can get me in trouble, but the opposite, "Herd Mentality," can also be problematic.

Example:

Mt. Vesuvius erupted 1,944 years ago. Today people have slowly crept up the mountainside and built homes. This is not good! It will erupt again!

One reason they do this is their idea of time. A few hundred years have passed, and, no boom! In Geological Time this quiet spell is like the time difference between a ping and a pong in the game by the same name. It's like the time space between the individual explosions when setting off a pack of firecrackers. Everyone else sees everyone else building on the side of this beautiful mountain. Be wise. Learn from others' mistakes, even if those "others" lived (and were quickly burned and buried) hundreds of years ago.

* * *

It's not how old I'm getting that bothers me.

It's how fast I'm getting old!

* * *

Equation? If everyone were to start getting
everything that they wanted

No one would get everything that they wanted.

* * *

If you keep using this: "Search"

You may start to lose some of this: "Brains"!

* * *

Where I am is important. What I do with
where I am is even more important.

* * *

What comes around goes around but
sometimes it's a very large wheel.

* * *

Therapy can be very beneficial.
When you go to a shrink, you grow!

* * *

We seem to be always running to something
but we are really running from something.

* * *

Hindsight is 20-20 but foresight is nearsighted.

* * *

Two kinds of fish. Salt water and fresh water.
They are similar but different. So are different
Anonymous groups from one another.

* * *

Erroneous consensus.

Yes, in some cases, the many can be going the
wrong way but they all agree they aren't!

. . .

In some cases none is better than
any! Rancid oil for example!

. . .

I'd rather die looking than stop looking and die!

. . .

When you prepare the soil for the plants, you know
exactly what you're going to do in advance. The
soil of your life ought to be considered carefully.

. . .

Multitasking, really?

One thing at once.

Two things at twice.

Three things at thrice, then everything turns out nice.

* * *

You can't get very far from the jeans you are wearing.

Same goes for your genes!

* * *

The human race is a continuous chain
that changes yet remains the same.

* * *

There is reality, and I don't want to see!

* * *

Nobody knows everything about everything but everybody knows something about nothing.

· · ·

There is no getting around certain things. If you want to learn something or change something, there is work involved.

If you want to learn how to be ambidextrous you have to use both hands.

The right hand can't teach the left hand what to do and versa vice…!

· · ·

I want to look for my secrets.

· · ·

Seeking the extraordinary but missing out on the ordinary worthwhile experiences.

· · ·

If you want to find out who you are, maybe start with finding out who you are not.

. . .

Instead of always having to settle and keep score why not just enjoy the game!

. . .

You don't need a toaster to make toast. Watch out for the subtle, the obscure that may be lurking about, or you might get burned!

. . .

Decisions, decisions.

Every decision I make does not have equal weight. Now, unfreeze!

. . .

We develop a callouses to protect ourselves
from getting hurt. Callouses protect, at the
expense of not being able to feel.

* * *

Once equilibrium is reached in anything—societal, political,
relational—there is a tendency to flow into *unequalibrium.*

* * *

Teens generally want to be distinct from previous
generations, dress, act, talk different, but
previous generations do the same, so they are not
different. They are the same. Now, if they did
nothing, no changes, they would be different!

* * *

Procrastination and worry are energy drains. The energy used rehashing an upcoming event or project could have been the energy needed to do it in the first place.

Maybe less!

. . .

Living well is the difference between an on-off switch verses a dimmer switch. With the dimmer switch adjustments can be made, because living well is realizing mistakes and shortcomings.

With the on-off switch, it's an unhappy and narrow life.

. . .

Wise when to admit,

you don't know if it was the lamp that blinked, or you.

. . .

There is a reason for everything, but what
is the reason for the reason?

. . .

Sometimes it's better to wade into a new project or situation.
When I dove into something I quickly dove right back out!

. . .

If a thought comes to me and I don't write
it down, forget about it! Because I will.

. . .

Too much drama leaves me Dramatized!

. . .

FIX IT TIME!

Some ideas are about as useful as gears without teeth.

Sometimes we go way too far in trying to solve problems.

It would be like finding out the roof is
leaking so we blow up the house.

That will end the roof problem!

• • •

Things we sometimes hear that 'offend' us can save our lives.

Things that we hear, agree with, and condone can kill us.

• • •

When I live in the freshness of life, I feel refreshed.
When I live in the stagnation of life, well, life stinks.

• • •

Let's not "Gloomerize" the situation.

• • •

I have to save myself first.

That's not to say I will not help someone who is in stagnation. I will offer them a rope or a stick to grab onto. I won't, however, jump into the cesspool with them. Then we would both be in the stink!

We can't save everyone but we can save some. Trying to save everyone can result in saving none.

Take for example a sinking ship where some of the lifeboats are in the water. There are people who already jumped overboard and this guy in a lifeboat is pulling people out of the water till the boat is overfull and in danger of capsizing but he has to keep "saving" more people in the water. What happens is the boat gets overloaded and everyone in it goes down.

Instead of waiting a short time for the next almost empty lifeboat to take care of the rest in the water, this guy tried to save everybody.

. . .

Usually I'm up and running.

Today I'm down and rolling!

. . .

In joy

Enjoy

May you be in joy.

*   *   *

In life, relax. Just don't be lax.

*   *   *

Having direction can be a good thing, a
compass instead of chaos.

*   *   *

I'm not obsessive! I'm obsfocuussed!

*   *   *

A psychological unconscious attempt at a fix may occur when one tries to find someone to attend to. An example is when a child's feelings are hurt by a parent, the child may go to their dog, and while crying hug and caress the pet while saying, "It's OK, it's OK."

Later in life they may pick a mate to "take care of" when in effect they are still trying to fix the hurt done by another.

· · ·

You shouldn't take something apart unless you know how and why it was put together.

That goes double for reopening someone's psychological wounds without knowing how to put them back together.

CONTROL

When the big things in life that are out of our control frustrate us, we transfer that frustration to the little things and try to control them, frustrating ourselves and the people we try to control.

∴

Give up, but be patient. It's like getting off a merry go round when you feel nauseous.

At first you feel dizzy, but you don't get back on to make it stop! Be dizzy a while.

∴

Some people spend a lifetime putting out fires, never realizing they are the ones setting them. They're the firefighter and the arsonist!

∴

Learning was a problem for me as I had a learning "different-ability." If they only knew, and knew what to do.

∴

Plant a seed but don't **overwater** or it will rot. So will a person if told something over and **over** and **over** and **over**… again.

. . .

Sometimes you are heading down a path and it starts to narrow and soon you are in the midst of a thicket with thorns. You have to back off of that path and get back on the main path even though you believe you're going in the right direction. Some continue on into more entanglements and pain because they set their course and of course it must be!

. . .

Didn't like it at First, and still don't like it at Fifth!

. . .

Blame doesn't get me off the hook; on the contrary, it keeps me on the hook. Hooked.

. . .

I used to have to have all my ducks lined up in a row.

Now I realize all I got was a bunch of "quackers."

. . .

If I knew what a PhD was at the time, I would have felt I needed one, so as to get through kindergarten that is.

. . .

Projection of an outcome can cause multiple painful experiences, without a shot being fired. An analogy would be someone standing in close proximity to me with a hammer raised.

If at the same time, I have a hammer, and every now and then hit myself in the head, I am *experiencing* a negative projection. As it turns out the person was looking and taking aim at a tarantula on the wall behind me.

Even if the person had ill intent I needlessly did multiples of damage to myself.

. . .

When things are going good (my way), I expect this
will keep happening and that it will even get better.

When things are going badly (not my way),
I expect they will continue and get worse.

All or nothing! One-way thinking.

"Exactatudinologists" suffer from *"exactatudinitus."* Not an
uncommon condition, but very painful to self and others.

One tends to pick apart everything down to the molecules
and atoms. It could occur when alone and observing or
reviewing life occurrences and situations, or as a tactic
used to avoid a question that may be uncomfortable
to answer because said party could be wrong and
or have to take responsibility for something. Dread
the thought! In such a case the questioned party asks
for further, more exact clarifications ad infinitum.

· · ·

Projecting the outcome of an event, whether favorably
or unfavorably, usually ruins the outcome because
it may be in conflict with your preconceived
notions, and after all, one has to be **right**!

· · ·

Mistakes

At times I have made the right mistake!

Once I thought leaving (or rather breaking away from) a girlfriend of mine was a mistake.

It turned out to be a blessing.

Only when I was returned to sanity could I see it.

* * *

I have opinions like everyone. If I say something that is not accepted or agreed upon, that's OK. I didn't have to ask their permission in advance to express it, as if I ought to have known whether they would like or dislike my answer. They can get over it, or they can get under it!

* * *

At what point do you stop telling your child, "Make sure you tie your shoes," because at first the child would sometimes forget? Does the parent continue to tell the "child" at year 1, 2, 3, 4, 5…10,15, 25, 30, 45…??? Stop it already!

* * *

MIM

Monumental Indecisive Monotony! Can't make a decision because it may not be the RIGHT one? It drives everybody crazy, including the driver.

. . .

Perfection! Really? Does perfection drive obsessiveness or does obsessiveness drive perfection? There's no perfect answer.

. . .

You can wait a very long time for nothing to happen!

Yes, waiting and patience are great. However, they don't determine the outcome.

. . .

Perfection Paralysis. Dicing and slicing words in an essay doesn't help one see the meaning of the whole.

. . .

It's not the meaning of the words. It's what the words mean that will bring about an awakening.

* * *

Can't get average daily things done if I put up the roadblock of Perfectionism.

I was like a tape player in the beginning. I had Fast Forward to the future and Rewind to the past,

I didn't have Play, which is the present.

* * *

Circumstances that occur outside of me do not "cause" my condition. Neither will they "solve" my condition. It's an inside job.

* * *

Obsessiveness may be an attempt to counter perfectionism. The belief that one has to do, act, and be right, exact, and perfect is debilitating and can lead to a miserable existence.

An obsessive state of mind seemingly appears to take control over the fear of and inevitability of being imperfect. The antidote is allowing in oneself the perfectly normal state of being imperfect to have it's way. Nothing to fight or win there.

* * *

Sometimes people keep talking and won't let go. They have a "lip grip" on my ear!

* * *

I'm catching up to life
rather than life
catching up to me.

* * *

GOD

There is the unknown. Sometimes the unknown can be useful. It is comparable to having a magical pie, with a crust that completely covers the filling.

Every piece you cut, great or small, is surrounded by the crust, so that you cannot see what is inside.

But you can taste it. You know it is there.

Like God

* * *

Life is **final**. Death is not; not as a Believer anyway.

* * *

Surrender. Get out of your own way, and go God's way.

Being "stuck on self." This is a problem. A solvent must be produced to remove this "*sticky sick*" sense of self. God is the solution.

Praying to a higher *self* is still "*stuck on self*." Have to **get the self outta here!**

* * *

Some people hate religion. They hate
Rules, the ones *they* don't like that is.

They are usually Rule-igious themselves!

. . .

Tire dressing

All shiny on the outside, with nails, bad alignment,
underinflated tires. I hid behind a smile and "everything
is fine" answer. Then I did some therapy and felt
better. More work, resulting in going too deep into
self, let me wear my non-shined tires on my sleeve.

Ask me how I was, I'd say, "You got an hour?"

Knowing too much is dangerous too. The cunning
part of it resulted in me becoming grandiose and
"knowledgeable." This can result in a "Higher Self"
belief, knocking God out of the picture. Self-discovery,
when taken too far, can result in self-absorption.

Face fear with God, on Gods terms, you win.

Face fear on your own terms, fear wins.

. . .

God Accompanies The Impulse

In the beginning I reacted to situations, not
knowing any better. Then, progressing,

I would react and upon looking back, realize my behavior.
I thought I could stop it now that I was aware of it but
to my dismay, I seemed to have no say in the matter.
Before I knew it the words or attitude was out there.

As of late I have noticed God working with me, side
by side. Just as the impulse comes up simultaneously
God has enabled me on several occasions not to
react and to feel serene at the same time!

That is why I need Him to remove my
defects, and I will continue to ask.

* * *

Now when things don't go my way I say, "Thank
you God." I learned that from experience.

My way isn't always the best idea.

* * *

Life may be "one long prayer." Once aware, follow directions and be receptive. Then, results follow.

. . .

The wind of God and fellowship keep the doors of remembering, gratitude, and hope from closing shut; from closing me back into me.

I need this breeze, always.

. . .

How to neutralize Spirituality

There is a force that wants to secularize spirituality. Yes, oxymoronic, but true. In effect this is a way to neutralize spirituality. If you can't beat the enemy, mate with it. The offspring will not reflect the original, thus destroying it.

. . .

To the agnostic or atheist,

God is improbable or impossible.

On that mortal mind

God looks down.

. . .

Some atheists and agnostics have nothing
to believe in so they believe *against*.

They believe in "Not God." They don't want any
hints of it around! Freedom or totalitarianism?

They want freedom *from* religion. Religious
and spiritual people want freedom *to*.

Freedom to practice and believe vs. freedom from.

It's almost as if some atheists want government-
sponsored atheism! Gee, wonder if that ever
existed. History shows the answer is yes.

. . .

Ordinary Miracle.

In fellowship, recovery is an *ordinary miracle*. Before
fellowship, drunks died, suffered, and were committed
to sanitariums. We may remain complacent
and ungrateful because we see recovery every
day. The extraordinary miracle is that the ordinary
miracle in fellowship exists for us every day.

. . .

We are not asking you to do remarkable things.

When you do the things suggested
remarkable things happen.

. . .

God with a capital G not small gods

. . .

It's easy to take the Lord's Prayer out of the Bible

It's hard to take the Bible out of The Lord's Prayer

. . .

Even though I have "free will" God can and sometimes will push or pull me, maybe give me a nudge.

* * *

New Age is the old age, repackaged in New Verb-Age.

* * *

Dying is a Hell of a way to go, if that's where you're going!

* * *

My connection is my protection.

* * *

It's about God caring for our lives if we will let God.

* * *

When your ego is up, you let your God down.

. . .

Without God in my life, I was the Captain of
my ship. It had no rudder and was anchored in
quicksand. I thought I was going in the right direction
and was secure until I realized I was powerless.

. . .

If I ask what God's will is for me about a situation
and I don't like the answer, I may be tempted
to ask again. If I get a different answer, watch
out. It may be the devil's will instead!

. . .

Confused. Refused. Agnostic.

Some people who are confused or refuse to embrace certain beliefs or understandings about life or themselves seem to strive at believing and having you believe there is nothing to believe. It makes them feel more at "home" with themselves and others, even though there is still no "home" for them.

. . .

Give thanks, praise, worship, gratitude.

. . .

Pray even after the fact!

It may help to pray for someone after they "got out of the woods" because God knows you were going to do it, even before you were born. But we don't know things beforehand. Doing a blessed thing even after the fact, may have brought forth the fruit before the seed.

. . .

God is not just a go to God!

He's a "give to" God.

* * *

What's all the stuff about "I don't understand God"?
You don't have to understand God. You just need
to know what God requires of us. It's like having
a car. You don't understand how it works but the
maintenance from the manufacturer says change the
oil, change the filter, etc. You don't know how it works
but you know what to do to keep it working.

* * *

Let God be the Great Exaggerator.

God can, for instance, exaggerate the "Laws"
of Physics! My God can anyway.

* * *

Sometimes I'm glad it turned out the way it didn't. My way!

* * *

Free will and God's will.

A guy in recovery eats a lot of cheeseburgers
and ice cream, and also smokes a lot.

He dies of a heart attack and goes to heaven. God
says, "Listen, why did you do those things? I had a lot
more people lined up that you would have met down
there, had you taken better care of yourself. Look at
all those guys you could have helped get sober!"

. . .

We are free to be unwise and stray from the ideal in daily
life. I don't think it comes with God's endorsement, though.

. . .

God, you didn't do it. You helped me through it.

You could have done it but then I wouldn't
have grown. Thanks for the help!

. . .

Confused? I think you talk to yourself too
much. Try talking to God some more.

. . .

Not ego powered but
God powered.

. . .

Trying to figure God out leads to figuring
God out. Out of your life, that is.

. . .

Is it God's will to ask for that job?

No, it's up to me to ask.

The answer is God's will!

. . .

Why do I attach sentimentality to past memories?

Sometimes I want to be like Mr. Spock in "Star Trek." I want to be free of certain feelings such as loss, fear of aging, of the inability to visit the time when I built and tinkered with little projects when 8 or 12 or 15 years old. Of those romances lost. Of people gone.

Spock! Shake me, wake me to the Now.

. . .

When in the preverbal frying pan of life,

God is my spatula. If I don't turn things over

to him he just might turn me over. But if I do turn it over, he will usually flip me out!

. . .

Keep it simple, but sufficient.

Some people can confuse the unconfused.

. . .

No one is important enough that they should take their own life but is important enough that they should live.

* * *

Are we a collection of experiences, beliefs, and ideas? We are more.

* * *

I'd rather be Saved than sorry!

* * *

Is it a co-inkydink, or when God winks?

* * *

SOBER THINKING

(A NON PROFESSIONAL'S IDEAS AND EXPERIENCE)

Generalizing alcohol as a drug may be a bad
idea. An alcoholic newcomer needs to relate
to alcoholic drinking and behavior.

* * *

Trying to use a Phillips head screwdriver
on a standard 1 slot screw doesn't work.

Does one say, "Well a screw is a screw," or "a tool is a tool"?

* * *

But I hear "a drug is a drug." Categorize it however
you want, but we are going to talk about alcohol.
Each group has the right to keep it to alcohol.

* * *

"Keep it simple" doesn't mean keep it insufficient.

* * *

It's like saying a language is a language. Well,
sorry, but I don't understand Swedish.

Or a disease is a disease. Well if I have kidney disease,
I don't go to a cardiologist. Or, I could go to a veterinarian
for gallstones, but I think I'll go to a human doctor.

If you go to a butcher does he serve you produce,
saying, "It's all food, and beans are protein too."

See, in that fellowship they specialize, and
are "experts," when it comes to alcoholism.

Let's keep this thing SIMPLE.

*   *   *

Serve up who we say we are.

Go to a real Chinese restaurant and
Tex -Mex is served? "It's food & hot!"

Go to a Spanish class and they are
teaching Swedish? "It's a language!"

No, they all specialize, and so it is.

*   *   *

It's like an oil change shop. Changing it prevents what caused your engine to fail the last time when you didn't change the oil.

But changing the oil isn't going to fix your burnt valves or leaky water pump no matter how many times you change it. It doesn't treat that.

Fellowship is not a cure-all! There is therapy, other groups, spiritual places, etc.

* * *

How can I win against alcohol? I lose every time. I fight myself. If I punch myself, then punch myself back, then do it over and over till finally I throw the last punch and knock myself out. Who won? I lose every time against alcohol till I understand I have to give myself up to a Higher Power. Then I win against alcohol.

* * *

Drinking turned out to be stealing from myself, my future, my wellness.

* * *

I drank when bad things were happening to me (poor me). I drank when I thought I was making things happen. Sad or glad, I drank.

. . .

Problem? Add alcohol and it increases, intensifies, and prolongs it.

. . .

You can quit with God's help. You can always go back with yours.

. . .

How long are you sober?

I'm sober as long as I practice some principles.

. . .

Lots of Time.

Everything else is secondary to that, in so much as what anyone thinks of me, be it highly, lowly, or "inbetweeny." My Higher Power who keeps me sober is who I'm judged by. That's what matters most. Look up.

* * *

The principles are in order because I was out of order.

* * *

Today is the best day to get and stay sober. If you wait till tomorrow

The unthinkable may happen

Think about it

* * *

little by little

whittle by whittle

away goes your sobriety

• • •

Drinking is like taking poison to cure the problem!

• • •

Feel trapped when sober? Drinking seems to
set you free but you get really trapped. So get
caught up. Catch the principles and be free.

• • •

Some of my deepest darkest moments happened
on bright sunny days, haunted by the dark veil of
alcoholism, where the light cannot come in.

• • •

Someday, it will *never* get better!

. . .

I can't take away your pain. Your pain doesn't have to take you to a drink. Not with God's help.

. . .

GPS

This stands for: God Powered Sobriety. It's my direction finder. It keeps me on track, and prevents me from drifting away from my primary purpose.

. . .

When I stopped believing in God, it didn't make Him go away. I turned my back on God but God didn't leave me. God stayed ever since I asked for help and did something about it a long time ago.

. . .

It used to be what my will was for God,
instead of what God's will is for me.

. . .

Powerlessness is similar to the Wolf Man changing and
succumbing against his will. The difference, however, is
the Wolf Man knows when the full moon is coming. The
alcoholic does not know when the next elbow bend, the
one that knocks down the first drink, is coming!

. . .

Powerless over not knowing when it will be bad
or how bad for how long, is powerless!

. . .

I have to Stop but I can't! I can only Go.
Sometimes Go gets stuck but it inevitably gets
back Going again and again and again…

. . .

Admitting you are powerless is like admitting your car has no brakes. Knowing that will not enable you to be able to stop. Oh you will stop eventually. Usually after crashing!

Saying sober on the one step? Nonsense.

If so, then it would be a one-step solution.

* * *

It's not whether you drink all the time. It's when you drink you can't stop and what happens to you. Eventually you will stay stopped less and less until there is no stopping! Then you'll say, "I used to be able to stop."

* * *

Keep bending your elbow.

Actually you can't stop bending your elbow. It's like quicksand: The more you move, the deeper you go. Might take a long while, or a day. You don't control it, alcohol does. That is powerlessness.

* * *

You can't outsmart yourself. You cannot get over on yourself, and alcohol will always win. It's like becoming a brain surgeon by cheating and you go to operate on the patient and he dies, except in this case the patient is you. You will lose against your alcoholic mind. Self cannot overcome this affliction. Shortcuts don't work. Playing the game, thinking you're getting over? Alcoholism wins again. Every step you take, it takes because it is you!

. . .

Alcoholic thinking-drinking-behavior.

The night before, at the bar, was a bad night. It led to arguments and resentments.

How could this awful mess get solved? Well, let's drink about it! That's the answer? Drink to solve the problems drinking created! It's "Genius Thinking" again, and again and again... Powerless.

. . .

I don't subscribe to the notion "I'm powerless over everything." That can be an excuse for sloth, victimhood, and apathy.

Let me say that I'm powerless over where the STOP signs are.

I'm not powerless over stopping at them, as opposed to stopping at drinking.

So I'm not powerless over everything!

* * *

Acceptance of the diagnosis and thereby the solution applied to everyone, except me.

* * *

I didn't accept it because I thought I was the exception. I wasn't ready to accept.

* * *

The first step is like the first stage of a rocket. It is not used to continue, only to start. If I stay attached to it, and don't move on with the rest of the stages, I'll fall back with it.

. . .

I can't get more time than I've got right now,
but I can lose the time I have, right now.

. . .

I thought feeling good was not feeling bad. Now I know not feeling bad is the start. Top that off with feeling good!

. . .

I do suggestions for a living, for without
them, I'm dead or worse.

The benefits are that it pays handsomely
and I can never get laid off.

. . .

There are two steppers, but also side steppers.

. . .

Long term sobriety: **Being sober long enough to know what to do to stay sober longer.**

. . .

I'm always one day away from a drink. That day is always today.

. . .

Suffering from early sobriety isn't permanent.

Suffering from drinking is, and it gets worse. Sobriety gets better.

. . .

"New or coming back?"

How about stayed. 8, 10, 15, 20, 30, 40… years?

. . .

You think people are being too pushy? They may be just nudging you… away from the cliff!

. . .

First I needed to observe that it works, then believe that it can work for me, then find out how it works, which has been already written down for me!

. . .

We always had a reason to drink. Now we always have a reason to go to a meeting. Use your imagination. You'll come up with one!

. . .

Start drinking after being sober for a while and you get back all the misery and complications PLUS INTEREST! Compounded interest too.

. . .

Popcorn is gonna pop and an alcoholic is gonna drink!

* * *

It's OK to have a mind, just don't let
your mind go to your head.

* * *

Isolating is crawling inside myself and that is not a way out.

* * *

My mind can't change my mind at all times.

* * *

Better to stay with the known that you know than
to go into the unknown scary place. Not.

* * *

Of myself, I am too much!

* * *

The Recovery Head Fake.

Think you're fooling everybody by appearing to
do well and going through the motions?

Fooling everybody? Fooling yourself! The Head Fake
will cause you headaches, lot's of different kinds of
headaches. The kind that come from drinking again,
because you probably will be doing that. No kidding.

* * *

Stay sober with help from H.P. and you get
better and better PLUS INTEREST!

Spiritual interest is the best.

* * *

Come to meetings till you come to, and you too can
achieve contented sobriety through taking a few steps.

* * *

If everyone says a little we can learn a lot. But if the few say a lot we can only learn a little. Share the time. It's spiritual.

. . .

We could drink over not winning the lottery. Every night!

Then if we won, we would drink over that!

Otherwise known as non-stop drinking.

. . .

It is said that we drank mostly for the effect.
True. We also didn't like the effect of being
sober, so we drank to get "UN-effected."

. . .

"Speaking"

I don't do it for a living. I do it so I can live.

. . .

God, you people, and me are most important. For without
God and you people, there won't be a me for long.

. . .

It's not Self Help. It's asking help for the self.

. . .

Like hot soup after being outside on a cold winter day, that
is what a meeting does for me. I feel warm and nourished.

. . .

Doing the suggestions in order gives one the
best chance of getting and staying sober. If you
want to take your chances, then don't.

. . .

As an alcoholic, drinking affects ones
sobriety. One can't stay sober!

. . .

A responsible non-alcoholic can lead a sober life. An alcoholic cannot. A Recovered alcoholic can.

. . .

God can't be "something else" or it isn't God, just a substitute.

Getting drunk, is not God. Sex is not God. A relationship is not God.

Those are fleeting. God is not.

. . .

I don't know what it's like to be sober for a few decades. I know what it's like to be sober in general. I'm recovered, and growing.

Can't wrap my brain around time spans like 10, 20, 30, 40 years. So I don't try. It's not what you think, especially when living one day at a time.

. . .

If I was asked, "Do you know what it's like
NOT to have a headache?" I'd think, well
I haven't had one in such a long time.

But if I had one yesterday, and today I don't, in that case,
yes! I really know what it's like NOT to have a headache.

Being sober a long time feels like the same condition
day after day. Feels normal, feels good. But in
the beginning it feels like no such thing!

. . .

What?! Are you waiting to get better before you
do a 4th and 5th? You get better by doing it.

Think about it.

Don't drink about it.

. . .

I know I have a tumor that hurts, so just knock me
out so the pain will go away. I wake up again. Knock
me out again. That's what I was doing. For us the
solution is surgery, that is, a recovery program.

. . .

"I can't unwind it."

When one crosses over into alcoholism they
never wind up becoming a non-alcoholic.

. . .

The mind that takes the drink can't outthink itself due
to lack of spiritual power. That mind is powerless.

. . .

When it comes to drinking, my limit is zero.
Have one and my limit becomes limitless!

. . .

Sobriety isn't like you died and went to Heaven.
It's that you lived and got out of hell!

. . .

Like trying to outmaneuver your shadow.

Shadow can go when HP shines over you.

. . .

TSD

Traumatic Sobriety Disorder. Newly sober can be traumatic. Suddenly sober after all these years is shocking, unfamiliar, scary, unknown. Like an ice water soak.

. . .

Now that I'm sober, things are starting to sink in.

When I was drinking, everything used to just float and soak!

. . .

Sometimes, when newly sober, things go our way and better.

But getting too much too soon can
soon lead us to the saloon.

. . .

An app for lower priced beer.

For free drink deals.

. . .

No app for sobriety?

The app is the application of Steps.

An app is a Program.

A suggested Program of Recovery.

So we have it!

. . .

No brakes! He drives anyway!

Stops when he hits something!

. . .

Towards the end of my drinking, I got about
three or four "*days to the gallon*"!

. . .

You soaked up plenty of alcohol. Now it's
time to dry out and soak up recovery.

. . .

I don't know about you but if you're an alcoholic and you're
not at least a little nuts, there's something wrong with you!

. . .

When I got a year, I didn't get it all at
once. I got it one day at a time.

. . .

The number of years counts for much, but

it's not just the number of years as what's

between the ears that counts most.

. . .

We do recover

We recover from not being able NOT to drink!

. . .

What is the symptom of an alcoholic? Alcoholism: repetitive, uncontrollable, continuous drinking. Drunkenness.

Recovered: No longer have the symptom. Still alcoholic, however. Picking up the first drink is the first stumble into the throes of alcoholism.

Recovered from the insanity of picking up the first drink.

. . .

There is at *first* Zero power. Zero power over drinking, and zero power over not drinking. Then comes the recovered part. Having the power, through our Higher Power (not you) to stay away from the *first* drink. So "*first* things *first!*"

. . .

Alcoholism is drinking, no matter what.

Recovered from alcoholism is **not** drinking, no matter what.

. . .

"Recovered Alcoholic" is still an alcoholic, meaning if he picks up a drink he will get to a place of what the dictionary defines as Alcoholism that is uncontrollable, continuous drinking. A Recovered Alcoholic by the grace of God is able to stay away from the drink, if he has a program that is followed. That is the Miracle. He has the power through God, God's power, yet he is powerless to control his drinking (hence alcoholism), if he were to start drinking again. Alcoholism is the symptom of being an alcoholic. Seek the solution and the symptom will no longer exist.

. . .

"Recovery" is a noun throughout this writing. If one is not yet recovered, then it's a verb.

Being "in recovery" is often used as a term for a greater fellowship and program of which one is a part of, as well as a state of personal change, renewal, relief from the malady, so to speak.

We don't recover from life. Remember struggling to stop? Remember being stopped but having to drink again anyway? Recovered is not having to, by the Grace of God, drink! Staying recovered is the final step.

"Still *recovering* after all those years?"

It's like saying, "I'm still recovering from my hangover."

But the last day you drank was over 23 years ago!

"That's the one."

. . .

What are you recovering from?

Have you recovered from drinking or are you still doing that? 'Cause that's what we're talking about.

. . .

Recovered means I don't have to do what I had
to do. I have recovered from the symptoms,
aka I am a *non-drinking* alcoholic.

C.S. is Continuous Sobriety. I stay recovered by
following a few simple suggestions, one day at a time.

. . .

Where does it say you're always recovering? Where
does it say we never recover? Quite the contrary.

. . .

Being restored to sanity with regard to drinking,
most importantly, is recovered from the insanity
of picking up that first drink. Again!

. . .

To stay recovered means total abstinence. That's what we
are able to do when we have recovered through steps.

. . .

Poison ivy. Still allergic. Now able to stay out of the woods.

◦ ◦ ◦

Not cured. Cured meaning drinking
normally, as in a non-alcoholic.

Recovered means NOT picking up that first
drink as a person who is still alcoholic.

Couldn't do that before!

◦ ◦ ◦

Recovered real. Relapse real. Relapse not required.

Stay recovered by maintenance of spiritual condition.

Not restored to non-alcoholic state.

Non-active alcoholic.

Restored to SANITY! No longer having "the mind
of an alcoholic" who of course, drinks because there
seems to be no available solution to the problem.

◦ ◦ ◦

Recovered! No longer in the recovery room. In there
it can go either way. They don't know. It's iffy.

Not with us! Rarely, have we seen a person fail to *recover*!

• • •

Stopping is the start.

• • •

Your problem hasn't been solved? The
one we have in common? Where we help
others to "recover" from alcoholism?

• • •

Instead of getting all wrapped up and intertwined
in a negation, just put a bow on it please!

• • •

If you're not ready to take steps, then you may be getting ready to take a drink!

. . .

It's a One-Way Drink.

You can drink your way into problems but can't drink your way out of them.

. . .

Everybody gets to have their first and last drink.

You can have your last drink by getting and staying sober or by dying a drunk.

. . .

Spiritual growth is one thing. There is also spiritual shrink. The slow slipping away till you take that first sip and maybe head into the abyss.

. . .

Shift

Some things shift, which is a form of change.
I went from bar hopping to meeting hopping.
Now I'm a regular at meetings! Shift.

* * *

Early on, more needs to be done. Damaged
goods need repair. I stopped getting burned from
putting my hand on the stove anymore but alas the
blister still hurts and the repair is in process.

* * *

Sponsorship

What an interesting relationship! Someone (sponsor)
who wants to control, but doesn't want to be controlled
trying not to control while helping someone (sponsee)
who doesn't want to be controlled but wants to
control! The fact that it works *is* a Miracle.

* * *

What a newly sober sponsee is really saying:

"I have an answer for everything."

How the sponsor is really responding:

"I have an answer for every excuse you have for everything."

* * *

Tell me what you honestly think. Not what you think I expect you to think. This way I know how to help you, like when a doctor asks, "Where does it hurt?" he can get an idea of how to treat you.

* * *

Let the sponsor "lead." Trying to guide the guide will lead us to both getting lost. The difference being that the sponsor can find his way out. The sponsee? Doesn't have a way out. The way in is the way out. So stay in!

* * *

It is suggested that men sponsor men and women sponsor women. Men have Spons-hes. Women have Spon-shes!

* * *

If these suggestions and sayings that sound "corny" to you work for others, then you ought to be all "ears"!

* * *

Getting and staying sober. Anything can happen. Staying drunk anything bad can happen and probably will.

* * *

If you think you can do this on your own, by not taking certain steps with others, then it's like you have training wheels on. You think everything is fine, till the curves come and the bike tips over. If you would have gone ahead and went through the difficult part, the fear of riding without training wheels, you wouldn't have tipped over. You could have done the opposite of what feels natural. Put the bike into the curve and get yourself out of the way.

* * *

Doing it "my way" may seem to work sometimes, and thus the illusion of control. Like sorting socks in the dark. It'll probably work a few times. It can reinforce the self-justification that "of myself, I am everything." Not!

* * *

You may have gotten help before. Someone may have thrown you a rope and you grabbed it. But each time you wait a little longer for help. One day you're up to your neck and it's too late.

* * *

I don't do "Program Lite." That will get me right into the drink. Heavy!

* * *

Fly Paper

The alcoholic is always attracting problems into their life. They figure if they can solve these problems, their lives will be better and they can drink successfully. The problem is that they are alcoholics and the problem to be solved first and foremost is their drinking.

They are like flypaper always creating and attracting problems. They need to become more like rice paper that doesn't create or attract problems. They need to change. Not that problems won't occur, rather they will be able to handle them. They will avoid the stickiness, the sickness of alcoholism.

Without a program, looking forward is the same as looking backward. The future will be a repeat of the past but with a difference. It will get worse.

* * *

If I turn it over, I don't have to do it over, again and again and again and…

* * *

I need a battery. I can't be the battery. If I keep thinking
I have power I'll be dead, like a Dead battery.

. . .

Albinos don't do well in the sun. Alcoholics don't do well
in bars. The albino doesn't sunbathe. But the alcoholic is
like a guy who goes out to sunbathe even with a sunburn!
Ask why? He likes it. Feels good! They can't **not** go out
in the sun! "Maybe this time I won't get burned."

. . .

An alcoholic falls into a hole in the ground.

Give him a ladder (assembly required) and he says, "You
want me to put together this ladder? It's got many steps. Too
much work. Just give me a shovel. I'll just dig my way out!"

. . .

Say same new, same new instead of

same old, same old.

. . .

If I don't show up, eventually I'll be throwing up. Again!

• • •

Some people go into mumble mode. I just
wait for the next person to speak.

• • •

Therapy is not for losers. It's for those who lost themselves.
Being a stranger to oneself is a lonely, scary, sad, business.

• • •

Sober. More sober? Sober is sober.

Water. Wetter water? Water is wet.

Quality of water? Polluted stream or fresh spring.

Quality of sobriety? Spiritual growth.

• • •

I think alcoholism and addiction have similarities that are different, hence specific fellowships for specifics.

* * *

You wouldn't use a tool that doesn't work. It could be dangerous. Same with your thinking!

Take it offline, your brain is broke, use someone else's, someone who has a good one, for a while!

* * *

I'm not a failure unless I pick up a drink.
In fact, if I fail to drink I am a success!

* * *

If I want something or someone,
but there's nothing I can do about it,

I'll do something!

* * *

It is better to embrace imperfection than
to try to perfect the imperfect-able.

. . .

You think it will start off the way you want it and if it gets
bad you can just stop. Everything happens in a day. It
takes just a day for something very bad to happen. Then
it's too late. A day can start by ending very badly. The
first one does it. Hopefully you will steer clear of it.

. . .

When we start drinking again we start not stopping again.

. . .

Forming fences for things indefensible is a waste
of energy. They get over the fence anyway!

. . .

Everybody dies but not everybody lives.
So live. The dying part is a done deal.

. . .

Towards the end I was sagging under the
weight of the burden of emptiness.

. . .

When the brightness and the awe become commonplace,
a feeling of the mundane may set in. You're not
a beginner. You just haven't finished yet.

. . .

I was trying to manage my life around
drinking and trying to act normal.

Really alcohol was my manager/employer.

But I was paying him, instead of getting paid!

. . .

I used to live to drink. Then I used to drink
to live. But it was dying, not living.

. . .

Stay centered.

Home base for mind and soul.

The regular home is for shelter.

. . .

Things got worse but as long as there was some light
I thought there was hope. Problem was the light at the
end of the dark tunnel was a train. It became clear that
everything was foggy. Time to get out of the tunnel.

. . .

I found that life is the greatest experience of my life.

. . .

Rowing on the sidewalk?

Don't work so hard. Get out and walk.

* * *

Drinking progression can begin by ending badly.

* * *

After a while, drinking starts adding to your emptiness.

* * *

There was a time when a "non-drinking" alcoholic was as likely as a fish that could not breathe under water!

* * *

I had the power to stand up

but not to the drink.

I had the power to sit down

but stood down

when it came to the drink.

Now recovered, God stands up for me

and the drink stands down.

. . .

My judgment gauge was faulty and
I read life as being a problem.

. . .

Managed to get drunk

hangovers

stomach sick, late for work,

couldn't work

car crashes

You managed? Alcohol was your manager.

* * *

Continuous drinking, sometimes punctuated
by periods of interruption,

always on a continuum of once again consuming more…

* * *

My car insurance is to take care of the
damage **after** it happens.

The recovery aspect is insurance to
prevent damage *from* happening!

* * *

LETTING GO

I hear you. It's difficult. Isn't it like being in a life raft and not liking the accommodations? You're going to land, eventually. Enjoy the ride and sightsee while you're at it!

For there is a sea of choking, suffocating, alcohol all around. Don't drift away. Nobody may be able to get to you in time, this time.

* * *

Some people go through very difficult, painful events during their lives. They are doing quite well in spite of the fact. Why? They go *through* it. The operative word being *through*. Yes, it may take therapy, prayer, and a mindset of living one day at a time, not in the past, not projecting a negative future, and not living in resentment! More on that to follow.

* * *

When on the ground an airplane's fuselage is supporting the wings. When in the air the wings are supporting the fuselage.

In the air we let go without even knowing it.

We are held together in a meeting by the group which consists of individuals.

We are letting go and letting a power greater than ourselves support us without even knowing it.

· · ·

Worriers don't have a future if there isn't one. Other than that, they will always be in business!

· · ·

Cast in plaster, once dried it's too late. If you surrender while the plaster is still malleable, then you don't ever have to get "plastered" again.

· · ·

There are certain times in our lives when circumstances or events bring us to a place of deciding to ask for help or continuing on our own. When it comes to alcohol, the time of hopelessness is the best time. Ask God to help you let go and give yourself to God.

* * *

Detaching is easy. It's the instant reattachment that is the problem.

* * *

Once I let go and let God it felt like:

A Calm Bomb had been dropped on me!

* * *

Change.

Like changing clothes.

Picture never having seen a washing machine.

First, admit the clothes you are wearing are dirty.

Then believe a strange looking machine can clean them.

The action is taking off the only set of clothes you own, hoping after you put them in the machine they will come out of the contraption in one piece, let alone clean. Or you can go back to doing it your way by putting yourself through the ringer. Again.

. . .

Lost in the details instead of found in the discovery.

. . .

Thinking has to be suspended in the beginning.

One day my car's low tire pressure light came on, so a tire must be going flat, right? I looked at the tires and didn't see a problem. I checked the tire pressure and it was the same in all four. So a faulty gauge that signals a problem is the same as my faulty perception of life when I'm new to sober thinking. My judgment gauge was faulty and I read life as being a problem.

. . .

Our best intentions can at times get
us in the worst of trouble.

. . .

It's a waste of time worrying about how much
time is or isn't left or has gone by.

While doing this worrying, one is using up time that would
have been better utilized in the endeavor called living!

. . .

I have to shut off certain people's rants when I start to feel like my brain is getting processed in a blender!

· · ·

Not admitting one has character defects/shortcomings is in itself the character defect of Pride. False Pride that is.

· · ·

Newcomers usually have 2 problems

1. They think.

2. Their thinking makes sense. To them!

Therein lies the problem.

· · ·

The loss of the drinking self

The old self is dying. It needs to die. Let it
go. You will mourn the loss. That's normal.

The old self wants to live. It wants to pull you down with
it. Do not yield! It is in its death throes. Give it a deep
burial so that you can begin a new life on the up side.

* * *

Loss of baby teeth: "Oh it hurts" and there is a missing
tooth! What if a new one doesn't grow? What's taking
so long? (faith) Who misses baby teeth? This is the
Step process: pain and loss bring on the new!

* * *

Sometimes I have to boil it off before I can cool off.

* * *

It's too much to handle, too much to
manage. Too much wiggle room.

* * *

Constipated Thinking

Ya just can't let the crap go!

. . .

An overactive sense of control example:

"Brace For Impact" before boarding the plane!

. . .

Let go.

Drop the Jell-O.

. . .

RESENTMENTS

Getting a resentment starts out with something that gets you angry, for example someone placing hot coals in your outstretched hands. The resentment starts when you reach down and pick up the same hot coals, saying, "Look what he did to me," while carrying them around, sometimes putting them down, and picking them back up, over and over, day after day, on and on.

Re*Zentments are Zents that we send to ourselves again, and again, and again…. It's like getting a nasty e-mail and forwarding it to ourselves so we can read it again, and resending it again, and again, and again…. One Zent is enough. It doesn't make Zents sending it over and over. It's non-Zents to do this. It's unrealistic to live in a Zent-less world, but possible to live in a re-Zentless one. Does this make Zents? On a good day I don't give two Zents, not even a second thought!

· · ·

TAFFY

Think Act Feel Free Yourself.

· · ·

Overwhelming! Some people can push, and push,
and try to sell you and convince you, relentlessly.
They may just be over-well-meaning!

. . .

Character defects are like flies swirling around me.
I know what they are but can't seem to get rid of them.

The problem is that flies are attracted to stink, as in my
"stinking thinking," which, once God helps me to do
away with, leaves nothing left for the flies to be attracted
to. When my Higher Power steps in through the steps,
I have a personality change sufficient enough to be called
a miracle. It's *removing* the stink, not perfuming it!

. . .

My Judgment Is My Jailer

When I say judging what I mean is condemning
as in drawing conclusions without inquiry and
staying irritated about someone not doing things
my way. So I am trapped by anger and resentment
about that which I can't control but want to.

This is different from discernment and using critical
thinking along a universal value system, for starters.
Then I use a moral compass to go even further.

* * *

Continually making negative noise will get you negative
feedback, either first- or second-hand. This is nothing
new it's just expressed differently. It is written "you
reap what you sow." So what did you expect?

* * *

Resentment leaves no room for me and God to occupy
the same space, the space between my ears that is.

* * *

Running to, or running from?

We seem to be always running to something, yet we are probably running from something. We need to stop, turn around, and face the fear; go through it, not around it.

. . .

Sometimes I reach "Aggravation Saturation!"

I need to remove myself from the situation

Without hesitation

Because I know my limitation

. . .

People say things they don't mean. People also mean things they don't say.

. . .

It's the resentment that dislikes and is disturbed. Not so much you!

. . .

Resentments can be dismantled. You
just need the right tools.

* * *

Let go of resentments.

Like a river that keeps flowing even though some
bothersome things come by, let them go.

* * *

A resentment grows when we build a dam
in the river and hang on to it.

* * *

Like dark clouds blocking the mighty sun,
resentments can block the happiness that is inside
you, but hidden under a cloudy, gray haze.

Accept, Forgive, Forget.

* * *

HUMILITY

The words human and humility start with the same three letters. Maybe humility is the 'ility' of being a human. Knowing our limitations and defects or falling short is quite humbling in itself. Our healthy dependence on others is good, and so is the want for humility. It's an ability through God. (the "ility" of being able).

* * *

Is he selfish? Does he want more?

Or, do I think I don't have enough?

A distinction of greed verses a real sense of insufficiency.

* * *

To inherit is through no fault, or merit, of my own.

* * *

It took the millstone much grinding to get this coarse chafe and wheat of a man turned into a fine flour.

* * *

My mind used to be a very dangerous and scary place to go. I needed a flashlight and a bodyguard to venture in there. Nowadays it's a very nice neighborhood because I avoid drama. Oh I'm still attracted to it but that's the point, I know better, I want an *average* job, girlfriend, life. It's the safest, most serene place to be.

. . .

If you always compare yourself to others that have more, are better looking, smarter, "more spiritual," etc., you will probably feel sorry for yourself and envious of them. The antidote may be to compare yourself to the "less fortunate" than yourself even if it is in your perceived terms. After all, these people may have solved the "happiness" problem through the humility solution. Or further investigation may reveal you are more fortunate than they seemed to be!

. . .

Perfection on the human plane would be, to say the least, boring, and at most, horrifying.

. . .

I'd rather be free of chaos and a slave
to boredom, than vice versa.

Boredom leaves time to imagine the possible
chaotic scenarios I could be involved in. That's
when I realize how lucky I truly am.

* * *

Just because I don't understand something doesn't
mean it can't be understood. Maybe just not by me!
Not at this time. Maybe never. Understand?

* * *

Either self is overcome, or to it, I succumb.

* * *

God is all powerful. I have to be humble. God does not.
I have to praise and worship the all-powerful God and
glorify God. After all, God gives me any power I have.

Also the power I do not have. That is

powerful.

. . .

I'm a member, though not in such good
standing, of the PTA Club.

Patience, Tolerance, Acceptance.

. . .

Our imperfections keep us humble. I'm grateful for them.

. . .

If you never heard a phone ring before, would you answer it?

What appears obvious to some is not obvious to others.

We aren't them and they aren't us!

. . .

I'd like to thank a fellowship' for letting me be
an idiot. I could have done it without you, but
I probably would have gotten drunk!

* * *

Thinking about all the bad things that happened
to you and the good things that did not?

Think about all the bad things that did not
happen to you and the good things that did.

* * *

It gets better too, or rather you do.

* * *

Getting out of self is still self-serving. What is the payoff?

* * *

I? We? I'm better off keeping it in the Wee i.

* * *

Am I doing something for someone else for a payoff?

Instead, what if I am doing something
for God and not for me?

. . .

Yes, alcoholics are experts. Experts at sports, experts
at running the world, experts at politics, experts
at mechanics, experts at running a mission to
Mars, and all from the helm of the barstool!

. . .

We have to clean up the past hurts, pains, and fears
to enjoy the now. It's like standing in a beautiful
field of flowers littered with garbage. It stinks! Clean
out the waste and smell the sweet flowers.

. . .

Better to over think things than to under think them.

There is excess to slice off when over thinking.

There is an un-sliceable absence of
substance when under thinking.

* * *

I'd rather be impressed with myself than

Depressed with myself. Overly impressed
or deeply depressed are danger zones.

That is not to say that feeling bad is bad.

It can lead to self-correction or finding
something incorrect in my thinking.

* * *

There would be nothing to see
if there were no incongruities.

* * *

DEVIL

The devil knows how to read. He knows Scripture
and is well versed in all fields of knowledge.

The question is whether one knows
what to make of what one reads,

for the devil is also a writer!

* * *

Being on the right train

There are many trains of life. They are all moving.
They all lead to the same destination, but beware. It
is the transfer station. Not the Final Destination!

* * *

You can probably buy ice cream in hell, but I can think
of better ways to cool off thank you very much.

* * *

Where that one is probably going, the heat and
hot water is included and the AC is always on but
never works. They're working on it though!
(Vincent Price laugh) Haaaaaa ha ha
ha ha ha ha haaaaaaaah!

· · ·

Some people know what is just, but
would just as soon *do you in.*

· · ·

The Enemy is also behind the lines; sneaks
in and makes out to be on your side.

· · ·

"The Devil is in the details" and once you start talking in detail all your life story with a trusted someone, the devil vanishes.

⁂

Shine the light on the darkness and it will go. You can't shine darkness on light!

⁂

TRUTH

It seems there is always one side to one side of the story.

. . .

Don't misjudge the poor soul

To assume knowledge of someone's character upon first laying eyes on them is akin to looking at the tops of their shiny shoes, not knowing about the holes in the "soul."

Conversely, the worn-out tops of someone's shoes do not reveal the new "souls" that have replaced ones that had holes. The shoes are now, shall we say, whole.

. . .

Take responsibility for behaviors. Don't say, "I was almost on time." You were late!

. . .

Jump and Judge!

Prior to arriving at a conclusion about anyone or anything,
or making a judgment call, an investigation is necessary.
Discernment is a necessary characteristic I need to develop.

Judging is healthy and not to be confused with
condemnation before a reasonable unbiased investigation
is carried out. That's why there is the word *Judge*.

• • •

Sprinkling an acre of good old-fashioned dirt with
a few grains of white sand does not constitute
a sandy beach. But this is the way truth is
distorted—a falsehood perpetuated as a truth.

A few grains of truth in a dirty lie.

• • •

Dust For Honesty

If you don't look for dust around the
house, you probably won't see it.

Then, on a nice sunny day you open the window and
a good gust of wind blows in. Among all the dusty
particles swirling around, getting in your eyes and
mouth, you utter," Look what the wind blew in!"

No, the dust was always there, in your house. You
didn't see it because you didn't "Clean House."

• • •

Clean, clean, clean.

Imagine doing the wash, but not all of it. You fold the clean
towels and a few unwashed ones and put them in the drawer
together! Then you do the same with the socks! A thorough
job of truth seeking is crucial in order to breathe free.

• • •

Muddy Wording

A twisting, vague explanation or answer, used
to try to obfuscate a spoken falsehood.

* * *

Sometimes I hear the expression let's go back to
basics. How about going Beyond Basics?

If there wasn't anything more, the word basic would
be unnecessary. Let's not forget the basics and let's
not forget more has come to pass from what has
been built on them. More has been revealed!

* * *

Beware The Rational Liar, usually
using illogical "logic" as in:

This therefore that:

All criminals are liars.

He lied, therefore he must be a criminal.

* * *

It seems we've gone to extremes. Somehow it is not okay to admit that people have their own set of values, experiences, and facts not necessarily separate from many other people's. It isn't "okay" to mention or stand for these realities. There seem to be many "pink elephants in the room" that we dare not mention for fear of "offending."

I believe we have entered "The Big Blur."

Things were clearer in the past.

· · ·

Sometimes I don't want to know "The Truth" in music:

It kills me when I find out the actual lyrics or some word in a song that I had wrong.

I liked it that way!

· · ·

Some songs

I don't care what is being sung

I just like the way it is being done

· · ·

No judgment? No discernment?

Why? So I can do as I please?

Paganism. Hedonism. Me-ism.

* * *

I think I wear glasses of which one lens is rose
colored and the other, well, skeptical.

Giving the benefit of the doubt is admirable
until I have no doubt (using discernment and the
other lens) as to the futile, probable outcome.

* * *

No judgments please!

It causes cognitive dissonance!

I like conformation bias!

As in the expression "It's all good."

Bullshit! It's not all good. There is evil also.

But good judgment takes work and thinking. It entails difficulty and decisions that may require action. Nope, "I just want to be Jell-O, grape flavor. Let me be Blob."

. . .

Reaching New Levels of Blurrrrr

. . .

Speech (and shortly to follow) thinking is becoming:

Homogenized

Sterilized

Neutralized

to our demise

. . .

Substance abuse is rampant. Many are under the influence, under the influence of thinking "substantial" thoughts, when they are full of hot air. Hence, claiming substance where none exists. Now that's Substance Abuse!

. . .

Feelings can guide us but not always lead us. Feelings could lead us in the wrong direction. Intellect ought to be mixed in for good measure, but If you're not getting it from the horse's mouth, you may be getting it from the other end!

. . .

Used to do this, used to do that.

Well, it's not used to anymore. It's now!

. . .

Seems like every time I have to deal with an
Institution, faith in my cynicism is renewed!

· · ·

Sometimes we have ulterior motives
we don't even know about.

· · ·

Why analyze the heck out of something you know is true?
If you don't like cilantro, so be it. Even if you found out
"why" you still wouldn't like cilantro and that's the truth!

· · ·

HEALTH

As a justification for eating poorly and indulging in a number of other unhealthy choices, people like to say, "*You only live once*," not realizing that before "the end" they could spend many years suffering from painful debilitating diseases and conditions. Yes, I know I only live once. I'd also prefer to only decay once. Preferably, *after* death!

* * *

I'm out here getting a moon tan.
It's very healthy, non-toxic, and pleasurable.

No sun screen or moon screen is required.

* * *

Product that works! This product really works but it is expensive. It's a skin product, a product for aging; aging conditioner. Use it regularly, daily, often. Use the product that costs a lot, ages your skin, and you. Smoke! You are the one who is responsible for the results.

* * *

We have to respect the body that enables us to use our mind and the mind that enables us to use our body.

• • •

The 3 F's

Fast Fatty Frightening food!

Cardiovascular disaster!

• • •

I have seen how chronological age can reflect vastly different states of aging.

No, age is not just a number.

• • •

Keeping my car detailed is a meditative experience. It can be soothing and enlightening. I call it The Car Chapel.

• • •

Sometimes when I feel like not doing anything, I don't.

Sometimes when I don't feel like doing anything, I do!

What's up with me?!

. . .

A man who was unaware of me was talking to himself as he entered the vestibule. We said hello, then he proceeded to turn the corner and I heard him talking again. I said, "He's talking to himself," but I said it under my breath, to myself!

That was a mental awareness awakening.

. . .

Dying is part of life they say?

Living is part of life.

Death is part of dying.

. . .

Cut down?

Stop trying to "abnormilize" everything
about yourself. Cut yourself a break.

. . .

JOKES AND... NO JOKE!

OK in all silliness… can we laugh at this now?

* * *

I know I'm getting better. My thinking used to be years out. Now I'm living in the recent future!

* * *

I think when the spaces between things in our body get bigger, and the things between the spaces get smaller, the effect is called old age.

* * *

Some people really go for a hike when they speak. They step on their foot and slip on their tongue.

* * *

Wash your fruit and veggies because you don't know what else the picker was picking when your food was picked!

* * *

It's good to be a little nutty, that way I won't crack!

* * *

Don't say, "Let's start from the beginning."

Start at the end, it's less stressful!

* * *

Someone at work told me she went to a flea market and bought a bottle of D.G. for $20.00 that was worth $80.00.

I said you better take a careful look at the bottle. It probably says Dolkhe Gabonsai!!

* * *

Vegetarian Newbee:

The furniture salesperson said to the new vegetarian, "This bedroom set is made with solid ma*hog*any." With a tinge of horror in her young voice she quickly exclaimed "I would never buy anything that had *pig* in it!" Well, he was hogtied by that statement!

* * *

To a well-read vegetarian, a rack of books is infinitely better than a rack of lamb!

. . .

People ask me to go the beach with them. I don't like going to the beach with them because I'm very "sand-offish"!

. . .

What's a woman who is always late called?

Delay-dy.

. . .

Every dog has his day. By no means do I mean that in a "derog-a-doggy" way!

. . .

If the doomsdayers are correct, when the world ends, I'm outta here!

. . .

When a recession is on, I decide that year
not to buy anything I have to pay for.

. . .

Multiple Relapser: I got another second chance!

. . .

Relativity always confuses me. Who's married
to whose cousin on whose side makes her
what to me? My relatives are relative.

. . .

When I was new, I was all Fogged Up!

. . .

If I want to be embalmed with 151 proof
Bacardi, is that a relapse? I wouldn't know,
'cause I'm dead! You guys figure it out!

. . .

If somebody gives me a resentment I just re-gift it!

* * *

You can trust me. Listen, I have no ultraviolet motives. I'm totally transparent.

* * *

There are some people I just can't face unless I look the other way!

* * *

Sometimes if you start to make a mistake, it pays to keep going!

Look how "tie dye" clothing started!

* * *

I'd like to prolong my life for as long as I live.

* * *

"Miss Understanding"?

I don't think she does.

I certainly don't understand her.

* * *

What is infinity minus one?

Close enough!

* * *

This guy is my hero:

I look up to the guy whose gorgeous girlfriend looks down on him. It gives me hope that I too could date a woman who is taller than not so tall me. This guy is my hero!

* * *

If you weren't taken I'd definitely stake my claim, with your permission of course, madam.

* * *

I am a proud member of this disorganization!

. . .

A.D.D. was not a disorder for me. No deficit here. In fact, it fit into my scheme of things. Attention Directed Differently!

. . .

I don't like being *prejumptuous*. I usually fall short anyway.

. . .

How many cups of ginger tea can I drink before getting gingeritus?

. . .

I used to be a Catholic. I find it interesting when people say I am a non-practicing Catholic. Is that like a non-practicing vegetarian? What are you practicing then?

. . .

Life for me is not as serious as it used to be. Seriously!

● ● ●

Lasagna is fattening.

It should be called "Lays On Ya" because
it tends to stay on ya!

● ● ●

Nun too soon!

Funny thing about nuns…. I met a few many years
after they left the order. I just couldn't picture
them de-nunified. I mean once a nun always
a nun in my eyes. She's come un-nuned?

● ● ●

Sexy dressing or dressing sexy

I mean, whatever is shown can and will be seen!

How could I *not* notice everything! That would
be like gazing into the deep clear blue water at an
island resort and *not* noticing the pretty fish!

* * *

I'm sure something I said sparked your disinterest!

* * *

X this X that.

People always refer to their X, as having done this, was
that, didn't do whatever, or was a you know what, etc.

Instead of referring to them as X, I like referring
to them as Y as in Y did I go out with them, Y did
they break up with me, Y didn't I think first, Y me!
So when I talk about my Y, now you know why.

* * *

I'm mechanically declined.

. . .

Let's all get sloppy stupid!

. . .

I'm doing two things at once so I don't
know one thing I'm doing!

. . .

That sounds very sar-caustic!

. . .

A friend told me about buying some cereal called
Ancient Grains. I said you better check the expiration
date. If it's more than 800 years old, I wouldn't eat it!

. . .

I think when Yin and Yang get together, you get Yonger!

* * *

Your nose can smell, but can you smell your nose?

* * *

He's not out of the woods. Just up in a tree.

* * *

My upbringing was my downfall!

* * *

Sometimes I get robo thinking. Can't stop the nonsense.

* * *

Sneezing uncontrollably, I asked someone
to call an anesneeziologist!

. . .

I wonder if cosmetic surgeons ever offer a 2 for 1 sale on
breast augmentation.
Or is that too shallow? Heck, that is exactly
what women are trying to correct. Shallowness!
So I don't think it's too big of a deal!

. . .

My brain has a deficit somewhere, but over
the years I've learned to work around it!

. . .

If there is nothing to do, then by all means, do it!

. . .

I missed my calling, I've been told. Serves me right for not getting that answering machine back in the day.

. . .

When I can't figure out whether to do something or nothing, I try a little of both!

. . .

The optimist says the glass is half full.

The pessimist says the glass is half empty.

The realist says it's a half a glass of water.

The alcoholic says, "I need a re-fill cause I'm going to re-empty this drink right now!"

. . .

Maybe some people are just lazycapped!

. . .

There is a type of atheist who suddenly, being convinced
of God, would summarily enact legislation against him!

. . .

This life will eventually be the death of me.

. . .

What's with this "**hands free**" stuff? Sounds like one is free
of hands! Smoke free means no cigarettes. Cancer free
means no cancer. So hands free ought to mean no hands!

Call it "free hands."

. . .

I was stung by a mob of synonyms. It was
shockingly electrostatical. A volt jolting buzz
of electrons all amped up. Ohms!

. . .

Diners were once very popular.

A local one, alas, has closed and
become another DinerSaurus.

· · ·

Instead of saying, "We need to have a *sit down*," which
sounds adversarial as in "sit down!" How about "let's have
a *chat down*," a kind of chat while sitting down. OK?

· · ·

"I heard you just retired. What are you going to do?"

"I haven't a clue but I'm reading books on the
matter. Never had the time when I was working!"

· · ·

They said pray for others, not yourself. So I prayed for a
miracle. I prayed she would get shorter, older, and not
as beautiful. I wasn't praying for myself to grow taller,
younger, and better looking so she would go out with me!

· · ·

I was very self-centered for a long time. I mean
to the point that for years I couldn't imagine
why anyone would want *self-sticking tape.*

Why would I want to stick tape to myself!

. . .

I drive myself crazy. It's the only way I know how to drive!

. . .

Some bras are so full and sturdy it would
seem to give her bulletproof breasts!

. . .

A guy like me is very "rigidmented." I think
I'll have to go see a "flexicologist!"

. . .

If I don't want to be single, I'd better start doing something about it, on the double!

* * *

BYOB? Yes…

In the 'rooms' it's:

Bring Your Own Butt

'Cause that's what you want to save!

* * *

People are always so busy that they have a difficult time just Being. I'm going to start an Adult Education course on "How to Do Nothing."

Of course the course will not cost nothing. It will cost something because Nothing costs something, or something like that, which will be taught in the course, of course. Yes, you will be paying for nothing!

* * *

Recovery

I just thought I'd stop by a local recovery group
to brush up on my public speaking skills.

. . .

Just thought I needed to go to a kind
of finishing school. Not!

. . .

Reality? I was finished! The real reason I "stopped by"?

To stop.

. . .

Beware of cults, or you may be
Cultivated before you realize it!

. . .

Early on we used to go to an after-hours place. After the meeting was over we went to the diner! We sometimes stayed there for hours.

I don't know about nowadays but in those days, diners were the "social media."

*   *   *

These things always happen sometimes. Yep…

*   *   *

You're all mixed up and confused and running in circles thinking?

I think you talk to yourself too much!

*   *   *

Cognitive constipation.

All thinking is backed up.

*   *   *

When under the influence (and sometimes in
between), things don't always appear as they are.
And things that aren't, sometimes appear!

. . .

Fake is the new real, as in implants.

How about a Fake Fetal Implant:

A woman gets a "try out" pregnancy before
actually getting pregnant for real.

An inflatable fetal doll, medically supervised to grow for
nine months will be implanted. Proper hormones will be
prescribed to simulate various functions, of course. You
can opt out at any time. There will be no refunds, but look
at all the money you save had it been real! No kidding!

. . .

When you come to a fork in the road don't sit on it!

. . .

At the supermarket checkout someone has toilet paper and says to the checker, "This is not for me!"

. . .

Chaperone: Hormone disrupter.

. . .

If I were a cactus I'd be happy needling you!

. . .

One heck of a health nut is the guy whose watching his house burn down and sobbing "my vitamins, my nutrients, my supplements"!

. . .

I got a restraining order against myself but wound up violating it numerous times.

. . .

I love life. I will prolong it as long as possible. As far as death, I will fight it off to the death!

* * *

I love getting even.

So much so that when my stomach growls I growl back!

* * *

I overheard someone say they passed the bar exam. Funny I have never been to a bar where I had to take an exam. They just took the money and I took the drink!

* * *

It's been said heavy drinkers can, with
some difficulty, stop altogether.

No wonder I couldn't stop. I'm a skinny drinker!

* * *

Some people feel deeply. So will you if they get angry!

* * *

HOPE

Hope is a condition of the spirit that pulls me through tough times and points me toward a bright future. It is God-driven.

* * *

Expectations are a condition of my ego and a selfish will that is finite and always hungry. It is man-driven.

* * *

Hope is wide and deep. It is requesting of. It is asking of.

* * *

Expectations are demanding of. They are finite.

* * *

Hope is better shared with others.

* * *

Expectations are the secret of self.

. . .

Hope will always find its way.

. . .

Hope is "the propensity to generate the belief in the possibility of my life changing for the better."

. . .

The alternative to hope is depression, darkness, death.

. . .

Hope is innate. A child is automatically filled up with it. A bright-eyed bushy-tailed look toward the next minute, hour, day, future, life!

. . .

Hope propels me forward.

So why dwell in the past? After all, there's no future in it!

* * *

Reasonable, limited expectations may run into
ruts and dead ends. Or they may not!

* * *

The Seesaw Experience

On the way down look up at where you will be. When up
in the air savor the experience instead of looking at where
you next will be, which is down. When down look up.

When things are looking up, savor the experience! Repeat.

* * *

It's so wonderful to know you are alive!
That you weren't always, and won't

always be, that makes living all the more precious.

```
* 9 7 9 8 9 8 9 1 8 4 8 1 1 *
```